God bless you!

GIRL SAINTS
for Little Ones

WRITTEN BY KIMBERLY FRIES

ILLUSTRATED BY SUE KOUMA JOHNSON

First Edition: December 2018

ISBN-13: 9781790593286

This book is dedicated to my daughters, Maria Rose and Lily Marie.
May these beautiful saints always guide and inspire you.

And to my husband, who always reminds our family:
"Our goal is to become saints!"

God would never inspire me with desires which cannot be realized;
so in spite of my littleness, I can hope to be a saint.
- St. Therese

St. Therese

Therese had a wonderful family. They loved Jesus and each other very much. Her father called Therese his "little queen." Therese wanted to be a great saint, so she did many little acts of love. Then, when she was only 15, she joined a Carmelite Convent. Right before she died at age 24, she said that she would send down a shower of roses from the heavens.

I will spend my heaven by doing good on earth.
— St. Therese

The hand of St. Therese's father is on her shoulder. He always loved her so much!

St. Maria Goretti

Maria was a good girl and helpful to her mother. However, her neighbor, Alessandro, was very mean to Maria. Because she only wanted to love God and do His will, Alessandro killed her. As she was dying, Maria forgave Alessandro for killing her. Later, Alessandro had a dream of Maria giving him lilies, a sign of purity.

I forgive Alessandro Serenelli...
and I want him with me in heaven forever.
– St. Maria Goretti

St. Maria is framed in gold, since she went to heaven as a martyr.

St. Cecilia

Cecilia wanted to be a bride of Christ alone, but she was forced to get married. When her husband, Valerian, saw how much she loved God, he became a Christian, too. At the time, many people didn't like Christians. Because she was a Christian, Cecilia had to go to prison. While she was in prison, she heard heavenly music sent by God. Eventually, she was martyred.

Put on the armor of light.

- St. Cecilia

When St. Cecilia died, she held up three fingers on one hand and one finger on the other hand. This symbolized the Trinity, one God, three Persons.

St. Clare of Assisi

Clare was the oldest daughter in a wealthy family. She loved to pray and decided to join St. Francis to live a life of poverty. She cut off her hair and wore a plain robe and veil. Later, she founded an order of nuns. Clare was very devoted to the Eucharist. Once, when soldiers came to attack the convent, she took the Blessed Sacrament to them, which made them run away.

Totally love Him, who gave Himself totally for your love.

- St. Clare of Assisi

St. Clare holds the monstrance up high as she looks up to her protector, God.

ST. ELIZABETH
OF HUNGARY

Elizabeth was a queen and loved the poor. Some people in the royal household did not approve of her helping the poor. One day, Elizabeth was bringing bread in her cape to the hungry. When someone from the royal household saw her, Elizabeth was asked to show what was in her cape. Suddenly, the bread had changed into beautiful roses!

How could I bear a crown of gold when the Lord bears a crown of thorns? And bears it for me!
- St. Elizabeth of Hungary

Since St. Elizabeth
was a queen and is
a saint, she has a
halo and a crown.

St. Philomena

Philomena, which means daughter of light, was a princess who, at 13 years old, vowed to give her life to Christ. However, when she and her father went to visit the emperor, the emperor fell in love with Philomena. When she refused to marry him, he put her in prison, where Mary visited her and told her to have courage. Finally, after forty days and many attempts to kill her, she was martyred.

Pray to Saint Philomena!
Whatever you ask from her, she will obtain for you.
- Pope Gregory XVI

St. Philomena holds an anchor and arrows because the emperor tried to drown her and then shot her with arrows.

St. Gianna

Gianna was a doctor, mother, and wife. She loved her family very much. However, when Gianna was pregnant with her fourth child, she found out she had cancer. She wanted to make sure that the doctor saved the life of her unborn baby, even if it meant risking her own life. After the baby was born, Gianna died of cancer, but her baby girl was able to live.

Look at the mothers who truly love their children: how many sacrifices they make for them.

- St. Gianna

St. Gianna is surrounded by pink and blue, baby colors.

ST. ELIZABETH

ANN SETON

Elizabeth loved to read. She was not Catholic all her life. After learning more about the Catholic Faith, she decided to join the Church. She wanted to teach others about her faith, too. She started orphanages and the very first Catholic school in America. Her life was hard, just like the cold winters where she lived, but she always wanted to follow the will of God.

Take every day as a ring which you must engrave, adorn, and embellish with your actions.

- St. Elizabeth Ann Seton

The beautiful rainbow colors in the window represent the dawn of the Catholic Faith in America.

St. Brigid

Brigid loved feeding and healing the poor ever since she was a little girl. When she would give milk to the poor, the milk would multiply. Later, she founded a monastery, many convents, and an art school. St. Brigid had a special woven cross, called St. Brigid's Cross. She first made this cross to teach a dying man about God and he then wanted to become a Christian.

I would like the angels of Heaven to be around us.
- St. Brigid

The flame
represents the
fire of God's
love in
St. Brigid's
heart.

St. Joan of Arc

Joan had a very important mission. When she was a young girl, she had visions of St. Michael the Archangel, St. Catherine, and St. Margaret. Joan said that they were so beautiful! They told her to drive back intruders from England that came into her country, France. Then Joan led the French troops to victory. Eventually, she was unfairly judged and was martyred.

In God's name let us go on bravely.

\- *St. Joan of Arc*

St. Joan looks forward to her mission as the Holy Spirit (the dove) guides her.

St. Kateri

Kateri was a Native American and part of the Mohawk tribe. Her family died from small pox and her friends made fun of her because she had scars on her face from the disease. But Kateri's soul was very beautiful. She fasted, prayed, and pledged to marry only Jesus. Because of her purity and love of Christ, she is known as the Lily of the Mohawks.

Look at this cross; O how beautiful it is!
It has been my whole happiness during my life.
- St. Kateri

Just like the green seeds in the painting, St. Kateri helped plant the seeds of new life in Christ.

ST. CLOTILDE

Clotilde was a queen. She was Catholic, but her husband, King Clovis, was not. She prayed for him and he became Catholic. After her husband died, her sons prepared to battle over who would take the throne. Clotilde prayed for them, which caused a great storm that drove the armies of her two sons from the battlefield. She spent the rest of her life caring for the poor and sick.

Hail, gentle and loving St. Clotilde,
sweet illustrious Queen of the Franks!

St. Clotilde loved helping the poor and orphans, teaching the people of her country how to be a Christian.

COLLECT THEM ALL

ABOUT THE AUTHOR

Kimberly Fries lives in North Dakota with her husband and three young children. She has an Elementary Education degree and is a stay-at-home mom and blogger. She loves teaching her children about the Catholic Faith through beautiful books and is excited to write many more. Find her blog at www.mylittlenazareth.com.

ABOUT THE ILLUSTRATOR

Sue Kouma Johnson lives in Nebraska with her husband. After earning her BFA, she devoted her time to raising five children. Now she has taken up her calling as a Catholic artist, painting saints and images that express her love for her Catholic Faith.

See more of her artwork at www.catholicartandjewelry.com and visit her Etsy shop at www.etsy.com/shop/TreeOfHeaven.

Did you enjoy this book?
Please write a review at Amazon.com.
Spread the word about my books on social media.

Want to learn more about my books?
And be the first to know about my new releases?
Follow me on Facebook at
www.facebook.com/mylittlenazareth

Interested in getting twenty or more books at a wholesale price?
E-mail me at mylittlenazareth@gmail.com

Made in the USA
San Bernardino, CA
03 April 2019